TUMBLEWEED 1

A Life Exceedingly Well Lived

Acknowledgements

I want to acknowledge the wonder lust upbringing of my youth as we quickly learned to be adaptive, flexible and nimble resulting from my father's job locations. My Father worked in a union environment and pursued railroad jobs to improve his pay and family benefits. Changes in locations, friends, conditions, and environments became normal. As you will notice in this book we relocated in our youth years preparing us three boys for our futures.

Thanks to Hal Watson who has helped with structural and methodology in preparing this book.

I want to thank my wife, Joyce, for the many hours of love, patience, editing and fine tuning this book. She gave me valuable feedback. This has been a very learning experience that will help in reducing future manuscript creations.

This book is an autobiography of Bill Marshall's life written by him, with interesting highlights of places travelled and worked in the world.

TUMBLEWEED 1

A LIFE EXCEEDINGLY WELL LIVED

BILL MARSHALL

Tumbleweed 1: by Bill Marshall
Copyright © 2024 by Bill Marshall
All Rights Reserved.
ISBN: 978-1-59755-815-0

Published by: ADVANTAGE BOOKS™

Saint Johns, FL USA
www.advbookstore.com

All Rights Reserved. This book and parts thereof may not be reproduced in any form, stored in a retrieval system or transmitted in any form by any means (electronic, mechanical, photocopy, recording or otherwise) without prior written permission of the author, except as provided by United States of America copyright law.

Life Application Bible

Unless otherwise noted, all scriptures are from the NEW AMERICAN STANDARD BIBLE ®, Copyright© 1960, 1962, 1963, 1968, 1971, 1972, 1973, 1975, 1977, 1995 by The Lockman Foundation. Used by permission.

Library of Congress Catalog Number: 2024950931

Names: Marshall, Bill
Title: *Tumbleweed 1: A Significantly Well-Lived Life*
                Bill Marshall, Author
                Advantage Books, 2024
Identifiers: ISBN Paperback: 9781597558150
Subjects: BOOKS: Biography / Autobiography
                BOOKS: Travel

Published December 2024
24 25 26 27 28 29 30 10 9 8 7 6 5 4 3 2 1

Table of Contents

ACKNOWLEDGEMENTS 2
1.0   TUMBLEWEED 7
   1.1 BLOWING IN THE WIND 7

2.0   A LIFE EXCEEDINGLY WORTH LIVING 9
   2.1 PREPARATION 9
   2.2 FORMAL EDUCATION 11
   2.3 YOUTH ACTIVITIES 13
   2.4 ADOLESCENTS 14
   2.5 ALGONQUIN PROVINCIAL PARK, ONTARIO 15
   2.6 RAILWAY DINNING CAR, PART TIME JOB 16

3.0   EMPLOYMENT 19
   3.1 CN/CP - CANADIAN NATIONAL/CANADIAN PACIFIC 19
   3.2 ARCTIC 20
   3.3 ROYAL CANADIAN MOUNTED POLICE 24
   3.4 CARIBOU 25
   3.5 RETURNING HOME FROM THE ARCTIC 26
   3.6 SOUTH VIETNAM- FIRST TOUR 28
   3.6.1 VIET CONG ATTACKS IN 1960S 28
   3.7 PLEIKU SOUTH VIETNAM 30
   3.8 SOUTH VIETNAM- SECOND TOUR 37
   3.9 DALAT, SOUTH VIETNAM MOUNTAIN TOP 38
   3.10 NHA TRANG SOUTH VIETNAM 41
   3.11 TET OFFENSIVE: "CHINESE NEW YEAR" 42

4.0   VIETNAM WAR IMPACT 45
   4.1 BOAT PEOPLE 45
   4.2 VIETNAM 3RD TOUR 47
   4.5 HAI PHONG NORTH VIETNAM 48

5.0   NEW WINDS 49
   5.1 ADOPTION OF A SON 49
   5.2 ADOPTED A DAUGHTER 50
   5.3 BELL CANADA TORONTO ONTARIO 53
   5.4 BELL CANADA SUDBURY 54
   5.5 BROADCAST CONTROL CENTER 56
   5.6 SBS WASHINGTON 57
   5.6.1 SATELLITE BUSINESS LAUNCH 57
   5.7 PLANO TEXAS 58

6.0   CHANGES IN LIFE 59
   6.1 OUTREACH 59
   6.1.1 DISCIPLES CRISTIAN CHURCH PLANO, TX 59
   6.2 PERSONAL CHANGES 60

6.3 NEW LIFE BEGINS 60
6.3.1 CAREER CHANGES 60
6.4 JOYCE 61
6.5 TUMBLEWEED IS MOVING AGAIN 62
6.6 AUSTRALIAN VACATION 63
6.7 GREAT BARRIER REEF AUSTRALIA 63
6.8 AUSTRALIA WEST 64
6.8.2 WELLINGTON, AUSTRALIA 64

7.0 FIRST ROUND THE WORLD CRUISE 67
7.2 HIGHLIGHTS OF FIRST WORLD CRUISE (2017) 67
7.2.1 CHINA, HONG KONG HIGHLIGHTS 68
7.2.3 99 YEAR ENGLAND'S LEASE IS UP HONG KONG CHINA 70
7.3 PERTH, AUSTRALIA 70
7.4 HOME OF THE KOMOTO DRAGONS 71
7.5 BALI INDONESIA 71
7.5.1 BALI WOMEN WITH FRUIT ON THEIR HEAD 72
7.6 SANDAKAN MALAYSIA 72
7.6.1 FAMILY OF PROBOSCIS MONKEYS. PHOTO TAKEN BY BILL MARSHALL 72
7.6.2 THAILAND RIVER LONG BOAT PHOTO TAKEN BY BILL MARSHALL 73

8.0 SECOND ROUND THE WORD CRUISE 75
8.1 ITINERARY 75
8.2 NHA TRANG, SOUTH VIETNAM 76
8.3 ABU DHABI UNITED ARAB EMIRATES 77
8.4.1 SUEZ CANNEL 79
8.4.2 CARGO SHIP IN THE SUEZ 80
8.6 ACABA JORDEN 80
8.7 ISTANBUL TURKEY 81
8.7.1 BLUE MOSQUE 81
8.7.2 ISTANBUL GRAND BAZAAR 81
8.7 SEVILLE, SPAIN 82
8.1 SEVILLE SPAIN 200-MILE RIVER CRUISE 83

9.0 CHANGE CAREER PATH 85
9.1 WE ARE ENJOYING OUR ANNIVERSARY 85

APPENDIX A 87
THERE WERE 29 HOMES IN BILL'S LIFE 87

1.0 Tumbleweed

I named this book Tumbleweed, because it reminds me of my 80 years on this side of the earth. According to Wikipedia, the Tumbleweed bush detaches itself and blows in the wind until it reaches a solid structure. It sometimes joins other Tumbleweeds. After spreading its seeds around, it settles down until the wind blows from a different direction and then it takes off again.

1.1 Blowing in The Wind
I hope you enjoy reading about my life experiences and the many places I have lived in Tumbleweed. At the time of authoring this book, I am 81 years of age, now that I look back on it was 1962 when my Tumbleweed detached itself from the root and started rolling.

One often hears the philosophy that life experiences can wait until I have less obligation, do not have the funds to travel, or feel the world is a dangerous place. We are taught to get a formal education first in life. But quite often the individual is not sufficiently mature to make the right choices regarding their educational needs. By the time they realized the early decisions were not leading them to the desired end results. Obligations have crept in, or funds were spent getting undesirable results.

I have made my share of wrong decisions in 81 years, but the path I have taken better prepared me for minimizing the heartaches and lead to a better future with God's plan. I have genuinely enjoyed the changes, and learnings from life exposure, failures, and successes.

Bill Marshall

2.0 A Life Exceedingly Worth Living

2.1 Preparation

I was born in Port Hope, Ontario, Canada. My mother, Edith Beatrice Marshall from Gainsborough, Lincolnshire, England and immigrated to Canada at an early age of sixteen. My Father, William Frederick in Lindsay, Ontario, during the Orangeman's Day parade on July 12, 1912.

My father, like my Great Grandfather, had flaming red hair. My grandfather was born in Ireland and was as King Frederick for his performance during the English Ireland war some 400 years ago. My Grandfather died 3 years after catching blood poisoning while working on the Bloor Street Viaduct in Toronto. My Father passed away on March 16, 1995, of age.

My older brother Frederick Lambert Marshall was born in 1937 at Kirkland Lake, In Northern Ontario's mining community. I was born in 1943 at Port Hope, Ontario. my youngest brother John Allan Marshall was born in 1947 in the hospital in Stouffville, Ontario.

My given name is James William Leslie Marshall. James came from my Uncle Jim Boe, William was my father, and Leslie was my grandfather's name. He was a sheep herder that migrated to Canada during the Potato famine in Ireland. He was born in Ballybay, Ireland. Of course, Marshall's the family name.

Bill became my name. My mother always referred to me as Billy Boy during my adolescence. On legal documents I was James William, and I became Bill Marshall as Billy Boy was not employed in the corporate world.

One of my early reflections is My Father's my Uncle Jim Boe showing me how to work a slingshot. I pictured myself as David slaying the giant Goliath.

My father's involvement in the Boys' softball league in Goodwood, Ontario was a challenge. One day, I walked into a steel swing at the playground and of course had blood all over the place. My father had to walk away from the ball game and take me to the Stouffville hospital for stitches. I recovered well, I think!

One of the good memories of growing up in Goodwood, Ontario, and even when we moved away, was spending time with our good friends, the Halls. Ted Hall and his family, including my first best friend Jackie, had a large dairy farm adjacent to our home. There are memories of bringing home the cows from remote areas at the time of milking. I discovered how milking machines worked, how to slop pigs and feed all the farm animals.

I remember when the local farmers would gather at the Hall's barn for the harvest to begin. Threshing in the fifties started with hauling in the threshing machine to the barn. Newt, an elderly man with a grease gun in hand, climbed inside the machine to lubricate all the moving parts. The leather clothing he wore was covered in grease.

A few days earlier, the grain was cut, and the machine spit out the sheaves. Sheaves are bundles of grain stalks gathered and tied with binder twine. The sheaves were stood up in the fields in 6 to 8 bundles per stook. On harvest day the stooks were gathered up with pitchforks and loaded in a horse-drawn wagon.

By this time, the one and only tractor was hooked up to the threshing machine with a belt, and the threshing was started.

The threshing machine shook the grain off the stocks and the grain was blown free of chaff. The grain was bagged, and the straw was loaded into the loft. The straw was also blown into the silo and made good bedding for the animals.

For lunch, the farmers' wives had cooked and baked a delicious meal. Jackie had planted a small garden, producing a prize size beet. His mother Eileen, prepared Jackie's plate by placing his large beet on his plate for his lunch. He had no intention of sharing his beet, so when the food bowls were passed around the table, they bypassed Jackie. When he complained he was told if he did not want to share his beet then the farmers did not have to share their food with him. This was an important lesson in life, that all can benefit from sharing.

2.2 Formal Education
Brother Fred and I went to a two-room schoolhouse in Goodwood, Ontario. I recall at an early age we moved to the country and the snowfalls were up to the telephone wires, yet we walked three miles to school each. In those days only the Model T Fords could make it through the snow.

I attended Public School in Goodwood, Waubaushiene, Cannington and graduated from Markham District High School, Ontario.

I started playing right-hand sports like hockey, baseball, golf, and football. Somehow, I chose to switch to a left-handed player while maintaining my right-handed writing skills. The reason was, I realized early that I could have an easier time being selected as an all-star team as a left-hander while most players were right-handed and faced more competition.

I graduated from Markham District High school at the age of seventeen and then went on to engineering school and graduated at age 19.

I graduated from engineering school at York University (RCC previously known). I attended courses in Toronto, Virginia and Texas. Many Real Estate and company management courses were also taken.

During my engineering courses, technological breakthroughs occurred such slide rules to calculators, and vacuum tubes to transistors and Integrated Chips. It was not only difficult for the students, but also the document writers and instructors.

Our world was constantly changing as I lived in twenty-nine different homes. We did move a lot as my father was a railway station master, and they are listed in appendix A. Frequently, we would come home from school to hear the announcement that we were moving. We boxed up all our belongings to get ready and to have our stuff put in a boxcar within another couple of days and get ready for the move, much to our chagrin.

My Dad mastered the art of multitasking as he could talk to us while sending or receiving a telegraphic message. He would then announce to the waiting passenger that the train would arrive in 20 minutes as confirmed by the previous Station Master. Prior to computers the world got urgent messages with Telegrams.

Many of the houses were provided by the railway and were drafty and cold in the winter. Us boys had a job to bring the coal in and keep the six coal stoves burning. One day a week we would bring out the galvanized tub and heat the water over the stove and each of us would take turns having a bath without emptying the water for the next person, of course.

2.3 Youth Activities

In Markham, I recall being sick in bed and telling my mother that I was ok and could go to school. So, she let me go but told me to be careful and take care of myself. Well, that was the day of the cross-country race, and I wanted to run. I ran and won the cross-country race. however, I could not tell my mom what happened and of course I was sick the remainder of the week. My mom looked at the yearbook later and saw my picture with a trophy and I had to explain my situation and beg for forgiveness. Of course, my Mom forgave me but was a little wiser to my tricks in the future.

I continued to go to school and work and as soon as I was 16, bought my first car, a Renault Dauphine. Getting a driver permit was a little easier as I drove to the local lumberyard which was awarded the Licenses. The guy must have been busy as he asked how I got there. I said I drove my new car by myself. He shook his head, and I drove off with my five-year driver's license. The car was a new model to Canada and the salt from the snow removal caused severe damages to the under-frame.

A friend of mine, Nelson, and I decided to take a short vacation to Sault Ste Marie on the Great Lakes. The roads were under construction due to their rough condition, finally my car gave out. The Renault rusted frame came apart and pinched the gas pedal, clutch and brakes. The roads were under construction and my car frame was fatally damaged.

Nelson and I had to figure out a way home. So, we tied ropes to the pedals, and I would push in, and he would pull out. It was difficult as the Renault was a manual shift.

As we drove up to the car ferry to Manitoulin Island, Ontario the crew realized that we were having trouble. The crew lifted my car manually onto and off the ferry. It was a memorable trip and the last trip for that car.

2.4 Adolescents

At age 12, while in elementary school I was busy picking strawberries by sun-up during the summer. I rode 4 miles each way on my bike from my home in Cannington Ontario. My boss asked me to stay on as he was cutting firewood that day. My boss Corm White called my dad and asked him at noon to come and pick me up as he felt I was falling asleep and could get cut up with the firewood.

My pal from down the street in Cannington and I used to do some crazy things. We would sit on fresh pile of telephone poles or railway ties as we enjoyed the creosote smell. We would sit there for hours and wait for time to pass. Today we find out that inhaling the smell of these chemicals, especially creosote, is harmful to the body.

We enjoyed flattening pennies as the train rolled over them. We made different designs with multiple pennies. Of course, we would get too close until it was a safety concern. Fortunately, neither of us lost an eye in our games.

One time we spent days designing elaborate arbors on our bikes to show in the summer parade. Neither of us found out the judging happened directly after the parade as we raced home.

The worst case was to come. My pal and I decided to camp out on a dried sandbar in a creek near the train tracks. We decided to pull the 6-inch weeds from the sand bed, or that was what we thought we were doing. We got hot and stripped down and jumped in the water.

My pal got a few itchy bumps while I got the worst case of poison ivy the Doctor had ever seen. They used to call poison Ivy the seven-year itch, but I had it so badly, I thought I would never get rid of it.

My schoolteacher came to see me at home after missing school for one week. She asked who I was since she did not recognize me. I had poison ivy where it was not intended to be. Eventually I got relief and returned to normal, just much wiser.

2.5 Algonquin Provincial Park, Ontario

In my teen years in 1958 My Brother Fred and I both enjoyed the outdoors. We took lots of canoe trips, camping overnight along the way. I have fond memories of camping out in Algonquin Provincial Park, Ontario.

Algonquin Provincial Park was established in 1893. It is the oldest provincial park in Canada. Additionally, since its creation it has increased in size and use to an estimated 2,955 square miles. It was exciting to see how the animals could roam free and enjoy the lakes and forest along with the campers. We saw moose, bears, deer, and many species of smaller animals. The bears have a night shift that allows for all trash cans to be reviewed. Accommodation varies from the ultra-nice to the camp-out sites. Fishing, swimming, bird watching natural habitat visits are popular activities.

My brother Fred and I went on a canoe trip during one rainy weekend. We chose to camp under the power lines in Algonquin Provincial Park. The snapping and popping of the wires kept us up all night in the mist and the rain.

The next day the river we had decided to traverse turned out to have a series of beaver dams. The industrious beavers figured out how make a pond for their families by blocking off the stream that flooded the area The did this with gnawing birch trees with their teeth. The stream was sufficiently blocked by branches to hold back water for the pond but to allow run off for the stream as before they started. This beaver project now had many uses such providing great homes environment for more beavers, places for animals to drink and play and a spawning area for fish. The dam, homes and food were provided by gnawing down birch trees with two strong front teeth. This is one of many God's ways of preserving the species.

The next day my brother Fred and I saw a large moose compared to a horse with a large rack of horns. The male moose called bucks would engage in mortal combat for the dominance of the females during rutting season. The top male bellow out to call the willing females to breed.

Two tired canoers headed home with wonderful memories.

2.6 Railway Dinning car, Part Time Job
During vacation and holidays, I would sign up as a Pantry Man on the next long distant passenger train. The duties were to help the chef, 2nd and third cook with the meals. I was in charge of tea, coffee and juices plus the breads. I washed the cups and glasses, small plates plus chip large blocks of ice for the water glasses. The waiters would give me their order and I would hand off the meal order to the cooks and ensure the 6 waiters had a full tray and their order ready, to deliver at the dining tables.

After a few trips I was promoted to a waiter where tips became a big inducement. Once I turned eighteen, I could serve alcoholic drinks. I put on a bow tie and a fresh white shirt each day and carried a try over my head with drinks and a meal, which is a trick on a moving dining car.

Tumbleweed 1

As many of the stops cross Province boundaries we could only serve beer from that Province. This created an inventory on runs from Toronto to Vancouver as we crossed 5 boundaries.

The Crew sleeping area was in a train car behind the coal car acting as a shock absorber for the rest of the passenger cars on the train. But the crew managed to sleep after the 16-hour workday. As a junior worker, I fell for all the jokes like getting a bucket of steam from the engine or finding a glass stretcher when the ice chips were too big for the glass. This was an early exposure to real life for a 17-year-old.

Bill Marshall

3.0 Employment

3.1 CN/CP - Canadian National/Canadian Pacific

The Canadian Railways were hiring Jr. Engineers to learn the Stock Exchange hardware. My first assignment was to repair the ticker tape machines. This was the stock exchange ticker display that is now shown in old movies. In the 1960s it was stale information where today you get instant information on your I phone. Also, today an investor can buy and sell stocks from wherever, directly with no need to call a broker.

I got a job offer shortly after this time for a position in the Canadian Arctic while I was graduating from the first railway training school. I gave my two weeks' notice and went to see my current supervisor for an exit interview. I asked him if I could return to CN/CP Railways when I finished my assignment in the Arctic with Federal Electric. My supervisor replied, "if there are ten jobs open and there were eleven candidates then my name would be the one we would toss out. Lesson learned in life, do not look back.

My girlfriend that I had dated for years, dumped me. She was not willing to have a long-distance romance, another lesson learned. I revisited her years later, but the candle was extinguished long ago. At that point all I had were the memories of "necking" and dancing to local bands playing "rock and roll" music. But I was starting a career job I always wanted with international travel and exposure to technical learning.

As a reader, fasten your seat belt as, my dream came true.

3.2 Arctic

I graduated in 1962 and commenced a full-time job with Federal Electric out of Paramus, New Jersey on a US Airforce secret assignment.

The mission was to identify enemy aircraft flying over the North Pole. I was assigned to a remote location with twelve people and spent two years there. I learned a lot about Radio Frequency-RF technology and had a good paying job. I learned how to deal with isolation and dealing with quirks that certain individuals had.

Part of the training was a course on weather. Learning cloud names, checking ceiling heights with weather balloons and practicing giving on-course weather reports to planes. This is knowledge I use even today during the evening news and weather forecasts. We used helium weather balloons launched before a plane was landing at the site to confirm temperature, visibility, and ceiling heights. Also, there were classes on the hardware and software to be used and supported.

The courses were held in a training center in a corn field in Streeter, Illinois. We were taught how to deal with the Arctic weather, including clothing to take for a year. We were told that a beard or long hair was not allowed on the DEW Line. The reason for this is the breath will freeze on a parka in the cold and pull the hair and skin off if you removed the parka immediately, once inside.

In the Artic Distant Warning - DEW, referred to as the DEW LINE there were 100 radar sites from the Artic coast from Tule Greenland to the Bering Sea in Alaska. The construction material was flown in with large aircraft on skies and large machinery dropped using parachutes. The entire DEW Line was installed and made operation in two year, a wonder given the complication in the world at that time and the hardships endured in the arctic.

It was a long flight to be arriving at the remote radar site. The site was a series of modules for the Computer equipment Radar control center, Station Chief, Crew bedrooms, mess hall and kitchens, libraries, camera film production, lounge and theater. These areas were connected with non-heated corridors so one moved quickly to the next module. The communication 60- and 120-Foot billboard antenna were mounded outside, and the Radar antenna sat on the equipment room second story. To round out the crew there were two power and an inside electrician. The radar antenna rotates 360 degree every 30 seconds with a lower and upper beam.

The power room supporting the site was in the large garage separate from the main modules site. There was a large rope going between main module to the power module and garage so that someone crossing the100 yard in a storm would not get lost in the heavy winds and blowing snow.

The most important feature of the bedroom was the blinds. During the summer months the sun remained above the horizon 24 hours a day. In the winter, the sun was below the horizon for 24 hours, so it was difficult to sleep, especially with a 24-hour job.

But nothing prepared me for the introduction to this new world. The trip from Winnipeg, Manitoba to Yellowknife in the NW Territories and Cambridge Bay on the Arctic Ocean was 18 hours on a 4 propeller DC4 airplane. The trip along the Arctic to the Yukon Territories was spent in a sleeping bag as there was no heat in the passenger area of the DC3, two propeller aircraft.

The touchdown was in an isolated site near Tuktoyaktuk, Yukon Territories. The living and work areas were modules sitting on stilts. Cooling coils around the piers to ensure the permafrost stayed in the ground for stability.

The Radar site and 60-foot antenna were impressive. We could see up to 200-mile radius on our radar scopes. This search radar was augmented by a ground level view through Doppler radars. We reported our findings to an Air Force command center in Alaska. If the intruder were hostile and unauthorized then the Air Force would launch an interceptor fighter jet to further investigate and take the appropriate action. Since the magnet North Pole and the real North pole had a 22% deviation above our site we had plenty of confused pilots to assist.

The North to South communication was from the Ionospheric signals and Tropospheric signals were used foe Eat West communication. If you think of imaginary belts around the world, the Ionosphere is the first belt inside the outer Atmosphere. The antenna direction from the earth, power levels, height above the earth are used to calculate the received signal strength. The bounce is the most reliable 180-230 miles distance away at the earth surface.

The Troposphere sites that carries the East to west communication, where the bounce is 80-120 use the Troposphere just outside our atmosphere. This 1950's Air Force technology, was soon superseded by an advanced Radar in the 1960's. This technology would bend the radar beam with the curvature of the earth and significantly extend the range of the coverage and eventually make the DEW Line obsolete in the 1990s.

The summer Olympics in Los Angeles, 1964 was occurring so our radar traffic had increased. The military flights to patrol the

Tumbleweed 1

arctic required in-flight refueling. It was interesting see the KC135 and bombers pull together as a hose was extended and fuel tanks on the bombers toped up and then both aircraft depart.

Each Engineer spent 4 hours per day watching the radar screens for unidentified objects and spent the remainer of the shift maintaining the equipment. The main assignment was searching the Arctic for enemy aircraft using the long-range search capability and dispatching speedy interceptor aircraft. The point-to-point doppler radar proved ineffective tripping the alarms with Caribou crossing the line of sight with the adjacent site. A migrating bird in the warmer seasons would also trigger a false alarm.

I recall one morning at 2:00 AM when it was still light in the Arctic, going fishing for Char. Char is a cold-water salmon that spawns and returns after 3-4 years to lay eggs. After the male fertilizes the eggs, they both die. We built a campfire to cook some fish, but the Eskimos ate raw Char as was the custom with the Natives.

We would invite the Eskimos to come in out of the cold for a movie. We turned the projector off after two reels. The odor became unbearable in the heated areas when they took their parka off. We waited until the air cleared before turning the movie back on. There are often few opportunities for a shower for the Eskimos in the 1960's.

The Canadian Government were concerned that was little educational opportunities for the Eskimo children. There were no local schools, and the parents could not home school since thy had never been educated. The Government Eskimo children were to be flown out to a government run school in Yellowknife. This seemed to work well, and the children learned a new lifestyle. The problem with the plan was the children brought their new language, culture, and expectations back home to their parents' displeasure. There was a difficult adjustment period for many years. The parents felt it was better to train their boys in how to fish and hunt. The girls were taught to skinny animals and sew them into clothing. The Children that were flown to Yellowknife and other similar schools acquired non-native desires, skills and tastes. To these kids a McDonald Hamburger was more delicious than a plate of blubber.

We were rationed six cans of beer per week. The beer, however, had traveled by barge down the McKenzie River to Tuktoyaktuk, thawing and freezing each day, then stored up to a year. The beer was a bit skunky, but we drank it anyway.

3.3 Royal Canadian Mounted Police
One day we got a knock on our door. It was the Royal Canadian Mounted Police from their island station some twenty-five miles away. They were on a remote assignment similar to us at the DEW Line only further north.

There was a growing fear that the Communists would attack the US and Canada over the north pole by land, sea and air. This was the Cold War days and the Cuban missile crisis when all children were taught to crawl under their desks if an attack occurred. This caused a generation to grow up with distrust of Russia and Cuba.

Anyway, their well-trained dog team had traveled across the frozen Arctic Ocean from their Hershel Island Command Post. This was a frozen island some 30 miles north in the arctic ocean. A single dog team on ice flows was very risky. I never did find out why they had come but suspected they just wanted to visit. They enjoyed our company and food. They showed us a polar bear hide that covered a regulation ping pong table with head and claws. I often wish I had bought it from them as it would make an enjoyable conversation piece in the future.

We had fresh vegetables and milk from the flight once a week if the weather cooperated. The RCMP got a flight once a month, so it was a very lonely place for them with only three people per military outpost. The flights arriving also brought us mail and news from our hometowns and the world around us and fresh movie reels. The aircraft that landed on the runway, had to be kept running when the crew came for lunch. Otherwise, the cold would freeze up the engine oil and prevent their take-off.

3.4 Caribou
The next summer the Caribou herds migrated past our Radar site. The Caribou were on a constant run for three 24-hour days, passed our site with over three thousand animals, followed by wolves. We closed the runway to avoid any air traffic to avoid any mishaps. This is done by issuing a NTAM- Notice To all Airman flying out of Alaska, Yukon and Northwest Territories in Canada.

We did resupply our meat locker periodically with fresh caribou. We had a Tech Rep from Texas that boasted he could also have a carbo and finish him off sharp knife. He did it and we hauled the carcass back to the site behind the snow mobile. The cook dressed out the caribou and froze it for future meals. The caribou is the size of a pony with big feet to allow him to walk on the snow in the winter, and the unfrozen top few inches of tundra in the summer.

A surprise was with short summer and the 24 hours the thaw in the top layer of tundra. This produced 6" tall flowers as far as the eye could see.

There were some unique rules about life on the DEW Line. I could take the bombardier or the snowmobile away from the site but always in sight of the installation. In the winter months if we ran into difficulty we could send up a flare so a rescue party could find us, so a second person was required in the bombardier.

Another danger in the arctic is ravine. These have been dug out by spring run-off and in the brief summer thaw will fill over with snow. The swirling winds would create deep holes in the ravines and in white-out conditions you cannot see the holes and the bombardier would fall in them. If this happens the driver or the passenger crawl to the edge of the hole and call the site for help as the signal would be blocked otherwise. This white-out condition occurs when the snow and the horizon blend into one color and the driver loses orientation.

A hobby I had with my camera was to use the dark room to develop black and white photos. Later I found it difficult to develop pictures in colors with temperature sensitive, multiple chemicals and patience required.

One of the excitements of the session was when the ice was pulled back from the shoreline and barges and landing crafts could resupply the site. These supplies were trucked into Fort MacPherson in the Northwest Territories and the, barges carried down the Makensey river to Tuktoyaktuk and to sites along the Beaufort sea.

We received our annual supply of beer, kitchen supplies, business and technical material and most importantly our annual fuel tank fill. It felt like an annual trip to Costco.

3.5 Returning Home from the Arctic
The plan was to take a short vacation after a year, but the DEW Line union was forming and Federal Electric my employer would not guarantee a job after leaving the Arctic. I delayed vacation

for another 6 months. I was a little "bushed" a term that mint you had been out of touch with civilization for a long time.

After leaving the Arctic, heading home our first stop was in Winnipeg, Manitoba. I turned in my parka and snow gear as I left for The Arctic in summertime 18 months prior. Upon turning in my winter gear. 18 months prior was summer, and I was not ready for the Winnipeg cold. I got a taxi to the Hudson Bay store and purchased the appropriate clothing. When I arrived at Toronto airport, I saw the oscilloscope I had built for test equipment coming off the plane, rolling "head over heels" down the ramp. My heart was pumping from the anxiety. Thankfully, it was well built as the scope worked well when I plugging it in.

The final observation after a year and a half in isolation was feeling uncomfortable during the drive home with my dad. The speed my dad was driving felt extremely fast. He told me I had withdrawal pains as I had not adjusted to the speed limit after an extended period of slow motion. I quickly solved that problem the following week with a trip to Acapulco, Mexico. After being there, one day I looked like a boiled lobster. The sun exposure on the Pacific Ocean beaches was extraordinarily strong. During the flight I met three brothers, and I was invited to stay at their Villa. One day we went deep sea fishing and took some beer with us. We did not realize how much we consumed until we arrived back at the docks and our legs would not hold us up.

Acapulco is famous for its cliff divers. The daring divers would leap off the cliff for a 300-foot dive into the ocean only to appear in 60 seconds from the surf below. I was continually asked if I wanted to go into a grass hut on the beach and smoke marijuana. I just had to turn around and look at what happens to people that took this drug and turned down the temptation.

I did go back to the DEW Line to finish my two-year contract.

3.6 South Vietnam- First Tour
In 1964, I was hired by Federal Electric to visit Vietnam as a tech rep working on an Air Force contract. This was quite a change of scenery and atmosphere going from freezing tundra to steaming jungles along the Equator. Saigon in Vietnam was full of "hawkers" selling all sorts of obnoxious food and the noise was a cacophony of sounds. In time the smells and sounds were acceptable as I got used to the conditions.

3.6.1 Viet Cong attacks in 1960s
I was assigned in the Page Communication Office in Saigon to the Pleiku Airforce base in Pleiku, South Vietnam. I had never been on an airbase, never mind one in a war zone. It was one jolt after another and at that age I was in a new world.

3.6.1 Vietnam War 1960s Beginning

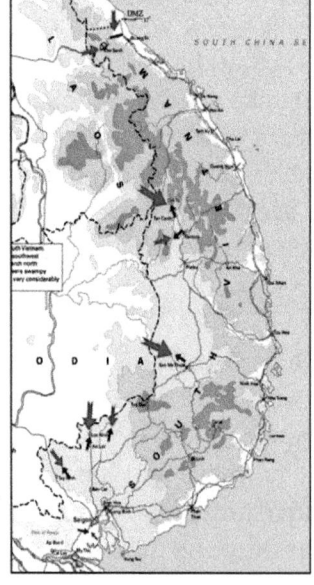

www.Britianica Free Grant

Tumbleweed 1

This was quite a change of scenery and atmosphere going from freezing tundra to steaming jungles along the Equator.

Sardine fish left in a brine and then drained off to make a clear liquid called Nuc-mum, a favorite Vietnamese flavoring. The first exposure to these smells and sounds was so foreign they were repulsive. But in time, they became appetizing smells to the foreigner.

Pleiku was in the mountain area beside Cambodia, near the Ho Chi Minh Trail. The Ho Chi Minh Trail was a series of tunnels and well camouflaged trails in the jungle. The trails ran from Hanoi in North Vietnam to areas around Saigon in the South. The purpose of the trail was to allow North Vietnamese Communist troops and equipment to be brought to the war fronts under the cover this trail provided. This supported the initial fighting between the North and the South Vietnam military. The South Vietnam miliary was quickly being modernized with hardware and training from the US. In 1964 steps were being take to bolster the fighting front with allies from Australia, Korea and other countries. But the North Vietnamese army was getting supplied with weapons by China. Their military had recently become experienced with jungle war fare in their removal of the French colonialist from their country and winning battles like Dinabandhu.

Here is what the Britannica described the run up to the 1960s in Vietnam Brittania Free The Vietnam War (TV series). "The Vietnam War was a conflict in Vietnam, Laos, and Cambodia from 1 November 1955 to the fall of Saigon on 30 April 1975. It was the second of the Indochina Wars and a major conflict of the Cold War. While the war was officially fought between North Vietnam and South Vietnam, the north was supported by the Soviet Union and China, and other countries in the Eastern

Bloc, while the south was supported by the US and anti-communist allies. This made it a proxy war between the US and Soviet Union. It lasted almost 20 years, with direct US military involvement ending in 1963. The conflict spilled into the Laotian and Cambodian civil wars, which ended with all three countries becoming communist in 1975.

After the fall of French Indochina with the 1954 Geneva Conference, the country gained independence from France but was divided into two parts: the Viet Minh took control of North Vietnam, while the US assumed financial and military support for South Vietnam. The North Vietnamese controlled Viet Cong (VC), a South Vietnamese common front of militant leftists, socialists, communists, workers, peasants and intellectuals, initiated guerrilla war in the south. The People's Army of Vietnam (PAVN) engaged in more conventional warfare with US and Army of the Republic of Vietnam (ARVN) forces. North Vietnam invaded Laos in 1958, establishing the Ho Chi Minh trail to supply and reinforce the VC. By 1963, the north had sent 40,000 soldiers to fight in the south. US involvement increased under President Johnc F. Kennedy, from 900 military advisors at the end of 1960 to 16,300 at the end of 1963.

3.7 Pleiku South Vietnam
I was shipped out to Pleiku, introduced to the military camp MAC-V (Mobile Army Command, Fifth Division) and assigned to a bunker and sleeping area. I also received a camouflaged helmet, a flack vest, M1 carbine rifle with a banana clip sufficient for 35 rounds. I complained that I was a Canadian Civilian, and I was given a "non-combatant" card in English with a hope the Viet Cong could and would read it before shooting me.

The US Army sprayed Agent Orange to kill off the vegetation on the trail to expose the Viet Cong. This turned out later to be very toxic to everything and the people in its path. I have Parkinson's disease today as one of the inflictions caused by Agent Orange. More on this to come.

The US Newspapers began to describe the war as the "Domino Theory" where the Communists would over run country after country if unopposed. When I arrived in Vietnam in 1964 there were 50,000 GIs in the country. In support of the Domino Theory as broadcasted by Radio and TV Journalists. When I left in 1968 there were 1,000,000 GIs in the country. The world was consumed by war and there was great opposition to it in the US. The World News focused on the body counts of the dead, daily. The US political situation forced people to take sides.

Riots broke out particularly from US students of draft age. This was the age of the "draft dodger," hippies and marijuana. None of which I participated in as I stayed focused on my goal to travel and learn my Engineering craft. During a lecture at the University of Toronto later it was revealed that at least 33% of the students were from the US and of conscription age. They had left the US to avoid being drafted in the military .They were referred to as draft doggers.

Amid this disastrous war Robin Williams produced a movie called "Good Morning Vietnam." While it has dramatic scenes in the movie, Robin Williams hit the nail on the head, with realistic descriptions of what actually happened. I strongly recommend this movie to everyone.

MAC-V had a large dining area, movie theater, PX-Post Exchange, hospitals, and bars. All designed for command and control of regional war activities within the 5th command.

As a civilian I have full PX privileges which means you could buy a carton of cigarettes for a dollar and alcohol for a dollar a bottle, and many other personal comfort items. Civilians could also use the post office facilities and select privileges around the camp. The mess hall which was right around the corner has my assigned bedroom. Initially I was quite excited as I was close to the dining hall. I learned that Viet Cong had attracted the complex previously. This resulted in stucco falling on my bed all night from a previous rocket attack. The cannon's bombing the Ho-Chi-Minh Trail go off every night and seemed like they were near. This shifts the plaster loose and it would fall on me including my bed. That left the room in desperate need of repair.

The "Chow" line had a box of yellow fever needles at the end of it. So, when you had both hands on your tray and before heading for your seat, an army nurse would give you a shot. I now had second thoughts about my decision to go to Vietnam.

www.flickr.com/photos/13411027@N00/
Grant (posted 28 March 2022 Steven Brown RIP

The AirForce continually had entertainment for the troops at Mac-V since it was a Regional Head Quarters. One night I could not sleep for the noise coming from the dining area. I got up and went to investigate. What I found was Matha Ray, who was a frequent celebrity guest of the military, entertaining. For the next four years she was a private performer for the military emphasizing her big mouth and gorgeous legs. She had previously been in a series of zany comedy roles. She proved to be a convincing romantic lead for Bob Hope (a longtime friend). This particular evening, she was holding a belching contest with the troops while consuming pitchers of beer.

The communication site that was erected and that we maintained as Tech Reps for the Air Force were impressive. These 120 Foot billboard antennae would eventually connect 60 Military bases in Vietnam, Cambodia, Thailand, and Laos. The configuration was similar to the DEW Line except for the antennas for each direction were massive. We were transmitting between 1,000 and 10,000 watts of power into these antennas. The first order of war was superior communications to accurately assess the status and plan the next steps decisions. In war decisions made by superiors without current and accurate information can lead to faulty orders to the troops that are executing these orders.

We had signs posted near the antennas of how dangerous it was to be in the path of the radiation, but I would see the ground keeper's crew hand cutting the grass in front of the antenna. I tried to warn them but the next week they returned.

Not all the local people were oriental Vietnamese. The Pleiku area was inhabited with Montagnard peoples. The Montagnard tribe looked more like American Indians. They originated in Mongolia Northwest of China. They were fierce hunters, with spears, bows and arrows. Their homes were on stilts to keep the animals from their families such as lions and tigers. They lived in the high lands and only associated with their tribe.

In time the US military gave the Montagnard men, weapons and ammunition to protect their families. A Montagnard village was 7 miles from our Pleiku site.

According to their customs, the women are bare breasted. The village women drew a lot of attention while they carried on their head, basket of trade goods for markets in Pleiku. This caused quite a stir among the American GI's.

This assignment was a valuable experience, as I continued to learn technology and eventually was assigned a management job at the age of twenty-three. I was given the rank of Lieutenant Colonel and promoted to area supervisor.

We received more civilian contractors along with US Air Force personnel to manage the sudden growth. Our temporary communication trailers were upgraded with steel buildings and our work became more organized.

The Tech Reps helped educate the Air Force personnel and many became motivated to continue their careers in engineering upon returning to civilian life.

The Civilian Tech Reps were offered upgrades to their on-based accommodations in the form of stateside house trailers. They were sandbagged for enemy protection. The base was already crowded so the house trailers were placed at the perimeter of the miliary installation. From the house trailer to the perimeter wall were mine fields so if one got turned around it was dangerous particularly if one was inebriated.

The continuous canon booms and the alerts that required us, dress in our military garb to climb into our assigned, bunker infested fox hole got old.

Tumbleweed 1

I soon got tired of the base life, turned down the house trailer offer and found a place to live in Pleiku village. I got a housekeeper and was introduced to my future first wife Lang. The installation of storage tanks on the second story of my new house and the shower head and drain on the first floor was a significant improvement. The housekeeper would collect water at a street access and carry two buckets with a wooden pole over the shoulder. It was a tedious climb to the second level, but the housekeeper did this trip daily in order for us to have a daily shower.

One day, the neighbors pointed out I had a butterfly with a 12-inch wingspan hanging on my front door. My neighbor, an elderly Vietnamese gentleman explained that this was a sign of good luck. I told him I hoped it was good luck for my safety. I furnished my new house sparsely, but I actually felt safer in the village than at the military base.

To ensure I had reliable transportation back and forth to work I ordered a Honda motorcycle. When my Honda, a 90 CC arrived from Tokyo I proceeded to Saigon to pick it up. I was not allowed to bring the Honda on the flight back to Pleiku, so I hitched a ride at the end of the runway on an Australian military flight with my motorcycle. I was strapped in along with the cargo and my Australian crew buckle me in on the tailgate.

The first stop was at An-Kay which was a military camp, still under enemy hostilities. The runway was steel matting, so it was a rough landing. The plane had to "Corkscrew" down to the runway to avoid enemy fire. It was then that I learned that the cargo was crates of eggs. The eggs broke and ran all over me and the motorcycle. After that, I had problems with mice climbing in my motorcycle and eating the wires.

Families with members in the Vietnamese military were most at risk from harm from the communist invaders. Families decided for their safety to escape Vietnam. They got to a US Military Installation, to a boat dock or to Ho Chi Minh International airport (Tan Son Nhat International Airport original name) hoping to catch a ride out of Vietnam. This was the start of refugee camps in Thailand, Philippines, and eventually the U.S.

There was an underground networks to support the North Vietnamese army. Many of the South Vietnamese families had family ties in the North from previous migrations resulting from earlier wars.

My Secretary, a fine gentleman with family ties to the North was receiving information on myself and my crew's assignment in Nha Trang. I held an office picnic at my villa in Nha Trang and we took polaroid pictures of the attendees. These pictures were passed around, but none were available after the picnic. After some investigation it was determined that my trusted Secretary was forming a dossier on each of us, and these photos were included. We found he was taking the discarded newspapers and periodicals such as the Time Magazines home in his lunch basket. Upon further investigation we found he was entering our compound through a local South Vietnamese guard at the back gate. I released him with the label Suspected Communist Sympathizer.

It occurred to me as I author these stories that God was with me all along. I felt ashamed that I had not recognized this fact earlier. Psalms 41: 2 says **"The Lord will deliver him in a day of trouble. The Lord will protect him and keep him alive."**

I volunteered for after-work activity at a local Catholic school and taught English to the students. The Nuns asked me to read to the student so the students could get the feel for a western accent. The kids would ask me about life outside of Vietnam and in particular about United States. I had a feeling they were asking on behalf of their families as the families contemplated becoming refugees and escaping out of Vietnam and constantly feeling the pressure of war.

I recall riding my motorcycle to school one day and noticed there was rice all over the road. The locals had blocked the road and dried their harvest on the paved areas. They were using rice stocks like brooms to sweep up the dried rice from the road. In time I learned to like the Vietnamese food and road rice.

After my first tour in Vietnam in 1966, I decided to return home to Canada. My father was always insistent on receiving updates once a week either phone calls or letters. I asked my Employer Page Communication if I could return via Europe. I receive a "round the world ticket" that had simple rules. Pan Am wanted the trip completed in a year, no repeat side trips and chose as many counties and stops as I wanted.

3.8 South Vietnam- Second Tour
Upon returning from a world trip and a Canada vacation I was told that I had a new assignment in South Vietnam. I was to construct Nortel Telcom services in the mountains near Dalat. I asked twenty more questions about the assignment and found out the last manager at the site and the employees were killed in a roadside incident. The Vietcong had placed Claymore Mortar explosives along the mountain roads. These explosives were set off as the crew drove up the mountain. All the Page employees were killed.

To prevent any further incidents such as what had happened, the military then offered a helicopter ride to the site every three days. Using the helicopter trip was a good temporary solution.

3.9 Dalat, South Vietnam Mountain Top

I needed the comfort of **Psalm 91:10-12** to sustain me "**no evil will befall you. Nor will any plague come near your tent. For He will give His angles charge concerning you and to guard you in all your ways**"

I discovered residential accommodation for the crew on days off in Dalat, so the Tech Rep shift was 4 days on and the 3 days off.

My crew worked hard to get the site on the air. Eventually, the Corp. of Engineers built log cabins to live in. The cabins were comfortable and had a large stone fireplace for cool nights in the mountains.

As the site Supervisor, I was provided with a Peugeot car for emergencies that runs to Dalat from the communication site. I sold my motorcycle at that point.

In the valley you could see the Vietcong army marching through the jungle. The U.S Army constructed protection walls and had cannon is set up to fire down in the valley and up the mountain sides if the Vietcong decided to attack the site. The rumor was that the North Vietnam military had Infiltrators within the South Vietnamese ranks and would use our systems to communicate war activities back to Hanoi. In many situations we could see the enemy and they could see us, but we did not disturb each other. The Army built a concrete wall around our site as we were exposed to mortar rounds landing on the roof and close by the site.

Our equipment was overly sensitive to shrapnel scattered from enemy motor rounds landing on the air strip near our locations. The sandbags around our wave guides (rectangular metal tubes to carry the high-powered Radio Frequency waves to and from the billboard antennas) were also a magnet for low flying objects in a war zone. The problem with sandbags around our waveguide was the rainy season in Vietnam. When the rain came the sandbag walls became saturated. With a minor wind or concussion from a nearby explosion, the wet sandbags fell on the vulnerable waveguide and caused an even bigger problem with our communication site. The only solution was to continue the wall around the communication site to include the waveguide. So, the Army came back and built a wall around all of our waveguide runs.

We had eight engineers working with the Air Force to complete construction and maintain the site. We were assigned ammunition and weapons for training purposes and a small Squad of US Air Force to guard the communication site. We also had a Philippine crew to manage the prime power set up as there was no commercial power. The Dalat communication site was on the mountain top and in time became a workable and livable location for the 12 civilian contractors and the associated Airforce and Army personnel.

Lang and the housekeeper would stay in the village of Dalat. Dalat was a vacation spot for the wealthy Vietnamese military brass. It had a 9-hole golf course and a great wet market for supplies. Dalat had a central water system and sewer system, paved streets, schools, and churches. After the War Dalat became a vacation hot spot for people around the world to go on vacation.

The French army during the 1950s used Dalat as their getaway in country vacation spot. The French were fighting the Viet Minh in Vietnam prior to the US involvement. The older South Vietnamese residents spoke French. Since I had rudimentary French in high school I was able to make conversation with the locals. This limited French proved especially useful in making Dalat contacts.

One day I heard about an Azzi flight that had engine problems. They had used the paved road a few kilometers from Dalat, so I drove out of town to see what was going on. The two engine Azzi airplane was in the center of the road. Fortunately, there was little traffic on the road.

The Azzis had set up a temporary guard around the airplane and was working on the engine when I arrived. I introduced myself and asked if the VC was around last night and they said nothing had disturbed them. I then learned that they landed the plane with one engine on this remote section of Road. The second engine had stopped, and a helicopter was on the way with another engine.

They planned to change that engine out right here in the remote area on the paved road. I asked if I could find them some breakfast, but they declined as they had eaten their C-rations. They seemed pretty independent and wanted to know what I was doing out there.

After a short while the copter showed up with the new engine underneath the helicopter. It dropped to the road, unfastened the new engine and fasten the old one to the ropes to the helicopter. They had brought a mechanic with them. I was surprised how quickly they had the new engine in place and were evaluating it. Very soon the Ozzie's were ready for takeoff. I helped clear a section of the road from accumulated traffic. It only took a minute, and the plane was in the air. I proceeded back to Dalat, happy that I was able to help.

One day after moving in the new sleeping quarters one of the tech reps was cleaning his weapon and shot himself in the foot. We called in a MEDEVAC helicopter, and he was taken to a doctor and returned later that day. He hobbled around for a week or so in that cast and finally he was able to walk again.

I invited myself one day to join the Filipino mechanics for lunch as they were having my favorite, fish head curry. Our mountain top communication site, a key role in the Military communication in Vietnam. So, we all sat around on the floor and ate our curry and had banter back and forth. Life on the mountaintop was returning to normal as one might expect as we shared quiet, and boredom interspersed with terror and lots of shooting.

All the Civilian Contractor we had no role in the allied, combat force. But at this installation because of the remoteness, we were invited to partake in their weekly practice shooting at targets. This was interesting as you got to experience all types of weapons including hand grenades.

My career in this assignment was growing with more responsibilities. I was assigned to a sector with six to eight sites to manage. I had to be relocated to Nha Trang on the South China Sea. I became very anxious to get off that mountain. I asked the military for a ride on a helicopter off the mountain. I went to the landing pad and waited and waited and finally called the helicopter dispatch, and they told me the helicopter had been shot down along with the district commanders and all had perished. Another sign that **God had been protecting me.** It was also revealed that I was to board the helicopter on the way to the battle area, but the flight manifest got changed to pick me up on the way to Nha Trang after the stop at the active military site. I fell to my knees after hearing this news.

3.10 Nha Trang South Vietnam
With my GS-13 rank I was able to bring my crew with me to the Nha Trang Officer's Club

One Sunday we decided to take a Sampan ride to Hong Tre Island about three miles up the coast of the South China Sea. The BBQ and refreshments were unloaded, and the truck left on the dock ready for our return. After a day on the beach and plenty of refreshments it was time to head back to the dock. The truck lights had been left on, so the battery was dead. The crew gave the truck a shove to get it started but pushed the truck over the BBQ in our inebriated state. The locals thought we were the "Keystone Cops." The next day we recalled the good times.

3.11 Tet Offensive: "Chinese New Year"

Permission Granted to use
https://legal.yahoo.com/us/en/yahoo/permissions/requests/index.htm

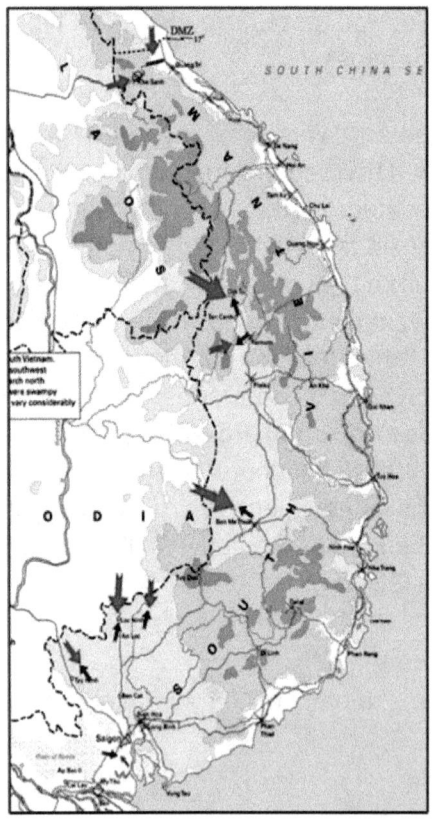

At the peak of the war in the Chinese New Year or "Tet Offensive" as it is called, erupted.

This was the turning point in the war. The Vietcong took advantage of the temporary peace in the war as the South Vietnamese military were sent home for the week of celebration. The following map shows how thorough the Tet Offense was.

The Vietcong invaded the country at the right time as the Vietnamese army went home for the holidays including the village of Nha Trang.

Fortunately, I had bunkers dug around our residential home courtyard and watched the Vietcong go up and down the street. After three or four day it was time to rotate the staff, so I talked to the base commander, and he assigned some GI's with automatic machine guns to get in my Crew Cab and we raced around town picking up the replacement tech's and taking the weary crew home. All this happening with no fatalities.

In fact, all my Tech Reps got off without a scratch and the communication gear as well. This safety was at all 60 sites which again makes me think somehow our communication was open to the communist. Giving them updates back to Hanoi in North Vietnam. Or could be the results of the dossier my fired Secretary assembled.

There was a tangled web of wires installed by the local phone service. It took years after the war for the technology and products we had available to us to reach the local infrastructure of Vietnam. To receive upgrades to their phone infrastructure required complete overhaul.

Bill Marshall

4.0 Vietnam War Impact

4.1 Boat People

The invasion from the North Vietnamese was turned back in a few weeks but the South Vietnamese spirit and hopes for a peaceful solution were dashed. The migration and humanitarian crisis in the south of Vietnam was at its highest in the late 70s and early 80s but continued well into the early 1990s. The term "Boat people" is also often used generically to refer to the Vietnamese people who left their country in a mass exodus between 1975 and 1995.

The number of boat people leaving Vietnam and arriving safely in another country totaled almost 800,000 between 1975 and 1995. Many of the refugees failed to survive the passage, facing danger from pirates, over-crowded boats, and storms. According to the United Nations High Commission for Refugees, between 200,000 and 400,000 boat people died at sea. The boat people's first destinations were Hong Kong and the Southeast Asian locations.

From refugee camps in Southeast Asia, the great majority of boat people were relocated in more developed countries. Significant numbers resettled in the United States, Canada, Italy, Australia, France, West Germany, and the United Kingdom. Several tens of thousands were repatriated to Vietnam, either voluntarily or involuntarily.

The Vietnam War ended on April 30, 1975, with the fall of Saigon to the People's Army of Vietnam and the subsequent evacuation of more than 130,000 Vietnamese closely associated with the United States or the former government of South Vietnam. Most of the evacuees were resettled in the United States.

In addition, up to 300,000 people, especially those associated with the former government and military of South Vietnam, were sent to re-education camps, where many endured torture, starvation, and disease while being forced to perform hard labor. In addition, 1 million people, mostly city dwellers, "volunteered" to live in "New Economic Zones" where they were to survive by reclaiming land and clearing jungle to grow crops.

Boat people had to face storms, diseases, starvation, and elude pirates. The boats were not intended for navigating open waters and would typically head for busy international shipping lanes some 150 miles to the east. The lucky ones would succeed in being rescued by freighters or reach shore 1–2 weeks after departure. The unlucky ones continued their perilous journey at sea, sometimes lasting a few months long, suffering from hunger, thirst, disease, and pirates before finding safety.

A typical story of the hazards faced by the boat people was told in 1982 by a man named Le Phuoc, (RIP). He left Vietnam with 17 other people in a boat 23 feet long to attempt the 300-mile passage across the Gulf of Thailand to southern Thailand or Malaysia. Their two outboard motors soon failed, and they drifted without power and ran out of food and water. Thai pirates boarded their boat three times during their 17-day voyage, raped the four women on board and killed one, stole all the possessions of the refugees, and abducted one man who was never found.

When their boat sank, they were rescued by a Thai fishing boat and ended up in a refugee camp on the coast of Thailand. Another of many stories is about a boat carrying 75 refugees which were sunk by pirates with one person surviving. The survivors of another boat in which most of the 21 women aboard were abducted by pirates said that at least 50 merchant vessels passed them by and ignored their pleas for help. An

Argentine freighter finally picked them up and took them to Thailand.

The boat people comprised only part of the Vietnamese resettled abroad from 1975 until the end of the twentieth century. A total of more than 1.2 million Vietnamese were resettled between 1975 and 1997. Of that number more than 700,000 were boat people; the remaining 900,000 were resettled in the U.S, China or Malaysia.

Brittanica free wikipedia.org/wiki/Vietnam War summarize damage the end of the Vietnam 1963 to 1973 The war exacted enormous human cost: estimates of Vietnamese soldiers and civilians killed range from 970,000 to three million. Some 275,000–310,000 Cambodians, 20,000-62,000 Laotians, and 58,220 US service members died. At the end the situation was desperate as would precipitate the Vietnamese boat people and the larger Indochina refugee crisis, which saw millions leave Indochina, an estimated 250,000 perished at sea.

The US destroyed 20% of South Vietnam's jungle and 20–50% of the mangrove forests, by spraying over 20 million U.S. gallons (75 million liters) of toxic herbicides called Agent Orange.

4.2 Vietnam 3rd Tour
It was now time to leave Vietnam as the conditions were unsafe. Toan and his grandfather caught a local bus to their home in the Mekong Delta, a safe area.

Mr father had written to me while I was in Vietnam and advised me not to bring home a Vietnamese wife. I never received his letter. My father said the letter got returned a month later as undeliverable. I felt guilty, responsibility, and compassion. I did not want to walk away from what I perceived was my obligations with Lang. I did not have a child with her or anyone else in my entire life. I lived with these feelings for 32 years. I had never failed in life with anything and was determined to make the marriage work against all odds.

I bought a home in Oshawa, Ontario, and we completely furnished it. I also went to the local GM Dealership and bought a brand new Camero off the showroom floor. But I still had that Tumbleweed feeling.

4.5 Hai Phong North Vietnam

When the opportunity presented itself I returned to Vietnam for a short work assignment, I took it. When I landed in Hanoi, Noth Vietnam, I hired a driver for my interpreter and myself to travel to the site in the morning.

All the bridges along the river to Hai Phong had been bombed and had fallen down. I lost count, but there were 10 to 12 bridges involved. To accommodate the necessary traffic, Bailey Bridges and ferries replaced the bridges. The US military was trying to disrupt North Vietnam war traffic from the busy Hai Phong port to and from Hai Phong. The two-hour trip took all day.

Once checked in at the hotel in Hai Phong we decided to go out and have some pho soup, an immensely popular Vietnamese soup. Along the street the food venders were selling BBQ dog meat, which is considered to be a delicacy in North Vietnam.

Hai Phong Harbor had been unmercifully bombed by US planes during the war and mines dropped in the harbor. By 1990 the bridges were being rebuilt and the mines began to be cleared. It took many years to rebuild the bridges to Hanoi from Hai Phong. The first cargo ship arrived at the Port of Hai Phong on September 21, 2021.

Tumbleweed 1

5.0 New Winds

5.1 Adoption of a Son
My first wife, Lang and I were introduced in 1965, and I was told her father and grandson lived in the Delta area of South Vietnam. The grandson was from a sister that had previously died, according to the story. It was now revealed to me that Toan was Lang's son. This all became known when I decided to adopt Toan and bring him to Canada and the Adoption Agency in Canada tried to get travel documents. Toan and I turned out to be best friends, but I never discussed the situation with anyone until authoring this book. There seemed to be no good reason at the time to announce this issue plus I felt betrayed. As it turned out, lying was a habitual problem with my first wife.

Toan became Tom, was brought to Canada in 1971 where he became an all "Canadian boy". Tom was quickly integrated into Canadian life and became a sports enthusiast. He played hockey, baseball, and football. He established himself on the playground and in life with enthusiastic involvement. Sports, school, and life were enjoyable for Tom. He graduated from High School in 1979 and started Oshawa College in Ontario shortly after.

At that time, my career was taking off again and Tom was transitioning to more involvement with friends, which got him involved in non-family activities. Lang and I found a hidden marijuana pipe and other troubling issues.

As Lang and I made plans to move to Virginia for my new assignment with Bell Canada International-BCI. Tom resisted the move! He wanted to stay in Canada and eventually rented a room from an older divorced woman. He became involved with his now landlord. We had less contact with him. I was paying his tuition at college but no longer getting progress reports. Finally, I contacted the college to find out he had withdrawn some time back.

Tom soon announced to us that he was getting married to his recently divorced landlord and was moving to Bellville, Ontario. The last contact we had with him was 25 years ago when we visited his new home and found he was happy raising grapes for sale as wine. He was not interested in reestablishing his family contacts with us, so we mutually have moved on.

5.2 Adopted a Daughter
Our first assigned daughter was on a plane from Saigon and crashed. We got a call from the agency that all souls on board, perished. A week later the Agency called and told us there was another flight of young refugees who were coming and that our daughter Kim would be identified to us. Next, we went to the Immigration place in Toronto to pick up Kim in 1973. The Agency had a room of Vietnamese orphans, and we were asked to enter the room and select our new daughter. I was not going to participate in the selection process, so the Agency introduced us to this malnourished toddler, and we took our adopted daughter home to Oshawa, Ontario.

Kim was very malnourished and had no memory of her early upbringing. Lang suspected she was an orphan from birth but, there was no record or history that came with Kim. I was spending more time involved with my career development and Lang was left in a new country to bring Kim up into an unfamiliar customs to both of them. As I look back now and can think about this situation it was very unfair to both Kim and Lang. Our intentions to help a war orphan were good but, the amount of time and care it would take was something both Lang and I were not prepared to provide.

I learned a valuable lesson in life that as a single contributor one can get through many situations. But in the new role as a husband, father, international worker on an aggressive job career life, solutions are much more complex.

Kim was struggling to fit into the family finding friends she desperately needed and at school. Fortunately, she shot forward in her physical self and became a beautiful girl. She outgrew her shyness and schoolwork started to come easier. She finished her education at Texas Woman's University (TWU) in Denton, TX. We came back to Texas for the wedding and Kim and Larry move to a new home in McKinney, Texas. Today, twenty-four years later I see on the internet that Kim has three good looking sons, and I am so proud of her.

At a later date Lang seemed relieved to be free from the daily demands of family living and our life together improved. However, the choices Lang made were to return to her Vietnamese culture and uncontrolled expenditures soon undid our love and trust for each other.

From the Dallas area I then took an assignment in Singapore. I had a significant responsibility for the Asian projects. I had teams to install a nationwide wireless system in Hong Kong and Singapore.

These were the first wireless communication in the world to work in the subway, road tunnels and steel elevators. Subway and road tunnels required leaky cable antenna installed along the restricted areas. The calls were passed along flawlessly to the next coverage area without the caller taking any action. This happened at speeds up to 60 MPH with Caller A talking to Caller B at 60 MPH in the opposite direction. Caller C) talking to Caller D) in another elevator was managed with an antenna in the top of each elevator shaft. Again, the calls were handed off to the station area flawlessly when the antenna allowed.

Just imagine a call set up when you get out of bed in the morning, connected to your called party from a cellular antenna in your car. Either caller or called party passing the call along on the subway train, elevator to your office desk, without dropping the call or receiving a bill from each leg of the call. Think of the productivity gained when your calls were managed in this fashion. You have earned your communication badge if you can visualize all this happening in the blink of an eye.

I had crews collaborating with the above companies to install optical systems.
A good example of the using a fiber optic ring to service remotely located students. Each group of students or individual student could have a centrally located instructor teach a network of students' algebra in a desired language. Each student will see the individual speaking through voice activation of the student or instructor in the ring. The program can be viewed by subsequent students with the previous students playing the role of instructor. This is a less expensive higher retention method of instruction rather than use of brick-and-mortar schools and a minimal number of paid inductors. Korea, Japan and the Philippians started this method of education 25 years ago.
I tried to visit a specific area of the country during my trips so that I could learn about the people and their culture. I called for a regional meeting in Manila, Philippians. Multiple countries sent their Project Managers/Representatives to attend. When the business items were completed, a bus ride was provided to Camp John Hays near Baguio City had been arranged with a guest speaker on the bus. This had been a US Military Camp during World War II and since turned over to the local government. The road to reach Baguio was along the mountains

on the coastline of the South China Sea. it was a treacherous road with sharp turns and narrow passages and cliff hangers.

A local guide/historian was our tour guide on the bus. He chose to talk about the Japanese invasion and the horrible crimes and battles that resulted when   General Douglas MacArthur took control of the fighting. He was a fantastic speaker and left you with images of the Japanese zero bombers taking out the US and the jungle fighting that went on. I felt sorry for the Japanese guests as this stirred up old feelings.

5.3 Bell Canada Toronto Ontario

I Joined Bell Canada in Toronto upon my return from Vietnam and was prepared to settle down. A Central office in Bell Canada was like a Museum of old vintages equipment that never got removed from service. Although the Central Office in downtown Toronto had the latest technology in compact solid-state equipment it also had to 70-year-old Open Wire Carrier with voice units 10 times larger than the new equipment. It also had the old test devices like a Wheat Stone Bridge to determine if a tree branch or anything was interrupting the connected calls. This presented an excellent learning experience for me. Some of the old times taught me all the vintages of old equipment that had vacuum tubes.

The new graduates showed me how to configure and make operational the latest solid-state equipment. Toronto had the latest Equipment it also had the oldest. Little did I know that I would use all this information for my next assignment.

As this was a unionized office all my fellow workers were upset when in a year I was promoted and made a supervisor. Our Director gathered everyone together and explain that I was young but very experienced with my Vietnam employment, so I never heard anything else about their grievance. I was told to go immediately to Sudbury about 300 miles to northern Ontario on the north side of the Great Lakes.

5.4 Bell Canada Sudbury

I was promoted to Sudbury Ontario. The Central Office felt like home as it was similar to Toronto, old and new equipment. Sudbury had very cold winters, but I joined the community leadership roles and learned again to enjoy myself. The community was looking for a sport director and I volunteered. I became the head snow shoveler for the outdoor rink, head of the wood burning stove committee and the umpire for the ballpark in the summer. I also played hockey at the 11:30 PM league, which was a drag getting up the next day for work. I also flooded the back yard and made a local outdoor hockey rink. In Sudbury it was far enough North that Ice stayed in the outdoor rinks for 3 months. I would often come home from work and turn a light on in the back yard, pull over a toque (some call it a toboggan) that covered the ears and head and play for hours.

I felt so restrictive after the life I had experienced thus far then I felt the Tumbleweed catch the wind and I needed to move.

My assignment with my buddy also a microwave route manager, Bill P, had maintenance people along the 1,600 miles of Ontario on the north side of the great lakes. We shared the route from Barry near Georgian Bay, Southside of the Great Lakes to Thunder Bay Ontario. As route managers we had maintenance personnel living along the microwave route with repeaters every thirty miles.

My engineers were provided with a Ford Econoline for maintenance equipment and travel to the sites. The Econoline had a snub nose front as the engine was between the driver and passenger. The driver's windshield was the start of the vehicle. If you "catch my drift."

Tumbleweed 1

I received a call late at night from the police that there was an accident. A moose was hit by our maintenance vehicle. The moose came through the front windshield into the back of the vehicle. The maintenance person survived, but the vehicle, moose and equipment did not.

These sites that we maintained were in a very remote area and, in many cases, were prime power sites with no commercial power lines. This was a very cold winter's night without power. Many sites have long drives that require major snow removal to get to the communication building in the Winter. Unfortunately, this site had lost both prime and backup power in the coldest of nights. The crew and snow blower truck arrived in the early morning and discovered diesel fuel had spilled out on the equipment floor and became a fire hazard. We later found a maintenance contractor had installed a fuel filter incorrectly and was causing the engines to vibrate violently and shake the parts off these power plants. This was big news of course since the interprovincial communication lines were all shut down across Canada.

In the Winter, these sites were accessed by snow mobiles. The next summer my Techs noticed sparks in the electronic room and upon checking further it was found that thieves had cut the copper ground wires. This wire was a ground for the site. The thieves sold the wire to a local scrap dealer. Since the replacement wires were exposed in the rocky terrain, we had cement trucks come and cover the new ground wires, so the threat of ground wire theft was eliminated and being struck by lightning was prevented.

We lived in a town called Blezard Valley north of Sudbury. Much earlier in time the meteors struck the rocky soil and dug a 20 miles long trench. Over the years the trench filled up with rich soil and became a great gardening area in this massive trench.

The meteorite was so hot in the earth it caused the minerals like copper and nickel to gather in veins in the ground.

The collision of the meteor and earth formed one of the richest copper and nickel mines in North America. These deposits were unnoticed in history, as this area is very remote in Canada. It was not until the area was cleared for train tracks in the late 1800s. The trees had been cut down and burned in a valley and the minerals from the meteor collision were exposed in the ashes.

The area made great notoriety in the 1980s when it was learned that the area was used by the astronauts for the first moon landing training.

The area was very prone to lightning strikes and with all the pine trees there were frequent fires. Once the fires were out the ashes made a great growing area for blueberries. This attracted the bears, and they developed the trick of waiting until the blueberries were picked, and the picker was scared enough to leave their baskets behind as they ran away. We eventually brought our dog along as our guard and that kept the bears away.

The smelting of the iron ore was such a generator of air pollution that a gigantic chimney was erected. It spread the pollution for hundreds of miles in the direction of the wind.

5.5 Broadcast Control Center
The next assignment was managing the delivery of the TV and Radio programing to cities across Canada. This was particularly interesting as Canada has six time zones with two major languages in addition to broadcasts in native languages.

Tumbleweed 1

As assigned to a new area, I learned the job by fire. I was the go between the broadcast networks and the ten provincial TV and radio control centers. The main Broadcast studios in Toronto and Montreal would send their live feeds to my control centers. The live feeds along with dozens of orders to send the programs via telephone Company facilities across Canada every half hour to seventy-five TV and four hundred Radio stations. The orders required the control centers to reroute the programs within a three second interval. It was a harrowing job with lots of pressure.

5.6 SBS Washington
I was transferred to consulting services on contract to Satellite Business Services in Washington DC. I headed up the Operational process and procedures for this new division of IBM. This was the first step of Nortel into the United State. I was sent to represent Nortel's launch of the Anik Satellite in Cape Canaveral. After two moves in the Tyson Corner area just outside the beltway in Virginia We had a new home completed on a small lake. It was a wonderful setting but in the flight path to Dulles Airport. We could watch the concord supersonic passenger jet, land from the UK in 4 hours.

5.6.1 Satellite Business launch
It was an interesting participation of two different established Corporations with their top personnel to integrate the latest satellite technology with new Client Companies from around the world. The target users were large uses of data voice and video while bypassing the local telephone infrastructure using satellite dishes on the roofs of clients. Canadian Resources were IBM's choice as there was good skills match and experience.

I headed up a team of 6 engineers to deliver our mission. BCI had approximately Twenty-five Representatives assigned with us to complete the telephony tasks. We would spend days working out operational interface designs, proceduralizing them and then instruct the new Satellite Business Systems employees.

5.7 Plano Texas

In 1988, Lang, Kim and I moved to Plano Texas. Before being assigned to Singapore, we decided to build a custom home in Plano. Our builder was a pilot with American Airlines and our neighbor. Before leaving for Singapore in 1996 we signed our contract to build while we were away. Our new home was to be ready when we returned from Singapore. It all worked out fine and the house was beautiful.

Back to Texas I established Nortel's Technical Support Centers CSC for Customer and installers to call for difficult problems to resolve. A Developer for each Nortel product was then brought online to assist in solving the problem.

Next, I was asked to head up a new project called FAST. First Application Test where new software and hardware was stressed, installers trained, manuals validated, and compatibility checked out with bugs fixes. The objective was zero incidents.

6.0 Changes in Life

6.1 Outreach
In 1974 I was asked as a newcomer to head up a long-range planning committee at our church in Plano, Texas. The committee presented the report to the Elders and the congregation and asked for their support to build a major expansion to the existing building. I was then asked to head up this next step as the building chairperson. The board approved. The Church leaders and the congregation approved the concepts for the growth as the first step. As usual, I knew nothing about what I was to do, but with God's grace I quickly learned the Tilt Wall Process.

6.1.1 Disciples Cristian Church Plano, TX
A tilt wall is a concrete wall created in sections and engineered with hook devices so the walls could be uplifted in a few days. The piers were dug as it suggested in the Bible. **Matthew 7: 24-25 "A wise man who built his house on the rock. And the rain fell, and floods came, and the winds blew and slammed**

against that house; and yet it did not fall, for it had been founded on the rock."

Two men from the church familiar with construction, took charge. On the designated day, a lift Crane arrived. The panels that were laid out on the parking lot in the shape of the church were raised and welded to the piers. A "Sweat Equity" program of church members did the finishing work.

It was with immense pleasure that Joyce and I drive by the church today knowing we helped bring additional members to the church with programs filling the new space.

6.2 Personal Changes
It was 1999 that I met Joyce. We were Deacons and Elders in the church and would serve communion and prayers to the shut-ins or elderly that could not make it to church . We also sang in the choir at Disciples Christian Church. We had no idea that God would connect us in marriage in 2001.

6.3 New Life Begins
My life was upside down and full of disappointments and feelings of satisfaction all at the same time. At the time I needed a partner as an anchor and someone to confide in.

6.3.1 Career Changes
Upon returning to Texas, I changed professions after major changes in my career path. After 32 years of engineering experience with Nortel, I began a new career in Real Estate. It was time to get off the "merry go round" I was immersed in. My affiliation with Nortel and the rest of its one hundred thousand employees around the world were advised that Nortel was going out of business. I terminated my direct support staff, packed my boxes and left the Nortel.

I opened my Real Estate Brokerage as BBS Realty at Robson Ranch. Robson Ranch was selling one hundred newly built homes, yearly in the city of Denton, Texas. They soon accelerated their business to building three hundred homes, annually. This created lots of demand for second owner and rental homes. This was a new career and right up my niche.

6.4 Joyce

Eventually I met Joyce who had also gone through a divorce. We originally met at the Church in leadership roles, Choir and Adult Sunday School. We spent long hours discussing our situations and it was a matter of diminishing one plan while growing another. I asked Lang for a divorce, and she accepted, and I asked Joyce to marry me. This time we both agreed that life was a "Wagon Wheel" with Christ the hub in the center to hold us together. We decided to make Christ the center of our plans. Joyce was the antithesis of Lang meaning she was the complete opposite.

We prayed that the qualities of each of our lives and our feelings be acceptable in God's plan for us. We have since grown in the name of Christ's promises and life has worked out well for both of us. We love each other and have done remarkable things for the right reasons.

Joyce and I made plans to travel to Hawaii for a way to rest. I secretly arrange a proposal plan on Wiki beach near a light house at sunset. When we arrived in Honolulu Joyce was not feeling well so we checked in and Joyce had a shower and went to sleep. I went out shopping for medicine to address her head cold. When I returned it was 6:30 PM and she was feeling much better.

We caught a taxi to Diamond Head. Just as I had planned the taxi found the stairs to the beach with the lighthouse. The sun was sinking, and I got on my knee and proposed. Joyce immediately said yes. My dreams were coming true.

There is a state law in the US for a mandatory period of months before you can re-marry after a divorce. However, in Hawaii the waiting period is 30 days. So, our marriage was good in the eyes of the law and in the eyes of God.

Next, I told Joyce about the plan to get married on the beach in Maui in two days and needed to get our Marriage License tomorrow in Maui. Joyce and I were married on the beach of beautiful Maui. We had a brief ceremony on the shores of the Pacific Ocean. We were standing on the beach with the wedding planner and the pastor and as soon as we said our I DO's we stepped back and a large wave came in and wiped away our footprints. I have often thought about that as a sign for a clean start and wiped-out bad memories of the past for both of us. Usually, I take time to analyze the situation and make the decision based on my conclusions and data (excel spread sheet) but in this case Joyce and I went with our gut feelings and now we know we made the right decision.

6.5 Tumbleweed is moving again
I had just retired early from my career in Engineering, got divorced, retired and looking for a new career. Now I moved my RV from the Plano area to Lake Whitney RV Park with Joyce. Joyce had an apartment in Plano after her divorce. She took the option to retire early after she was diagnosed with breast cancer in 2000. We had to make plans for the new life and reset previous plans. We now had a plan to build an RV home at Lake Whitney and purchased a large building lot.

We had a pontoon boat and had memorable times on Lake Whitney. One of those times that sticks in my mind was when Reagan our granddaughter was about 9 months old. We took the boat out one evening for a bar-be-que and a little fishing. She was too small to just crawl around on the deck, so we turned a large igloo (ice chest) into a small pool for her to play in.

6.6 Australian Vacation

Joyce and I needed a vacation, and I wanted to show her the Gold Coast and the Great Barrier Reef in Australia.

Joyce and I took the long flight from Dallas, Texas to Sydney, Australia. We had reservations for a camper and quickly found a park to camp overnight. Joyce immediately fell into bed, while I was trying to start a campfire.

Soon, there were hundreds of pretty parrots sitting on my head, shoulders, knees, and my arms, they were all over me. They were obviously looking for handouts, but they were a colorful delight and a welcome to Sydney.

The next as we drove along past the ocean in Queenstown, we saw roadkill Kangaroos but not live ones. The next day we decided to play golf, The golf course had all the Kangaroos we had been missing.

The Aboriginals showed us unusual ways they prepare kangaroos meat to eat. We continued to travel up the Gold Coast and eventually got to the Great Barrier Reef. It was spectacular the world underneath us at the Great Barrier.

6.7 Great Barrier Reef Australia

The Great Barrier is the largest area of coral reef in the world. Unfortunately, it is dying off today because of the rising temperature in the sea. Of particular interest with the little crabs that would congregate in an area and lose their shells and then take off in different directions for new shells to grow. The diverse types of coral cover the reef for one-hundred thirty-three thousand square miles.

We spent time in Sydney and went to the Opera House, one of the famous sites of the world.

6.8 Australia West

6.81 Burnie, Australia is the fourth largest city in Tasmania, Australia, serving as a major port for north-western agricultural and mining industries.

I became interested in Wombats and wanted to share information on this little unknown and interesting animal with you. They are herbivores and feed on grass, roots of shrubs and trees and fungi. They can graze for up to 8 hours a night and travel quite far from their burrows in search of food. Wombats' burrower and will dig out tunnels measuring 100 feet long. They live a solitary life in these burrows.

The wombat farts a lot and their poop is square so that they can deposit their signs on rocks that will not run off in a rainstorm. The wombat lives longer than the koala bear and in some cases can live up to thirty years of age.

6.8.2 Wellington, Australia
A town located in the New South Wales region of Australia. Wellington was the second European settlement west of the Blue Mountains. It was the first to establish as a convict jail in 1823. The city still has a strong Aboriginal presence. Largely as a result of early missionary settlements In 1907 a group of Wiradjuri people were awarded a Native title.

6.8.3 Mob of Kangaroo A fully grown male kangaroo may weigh up to 200 pounds and reach 6 foot 7 inches in length. With a deadly kick to the human body. The kangaroo and the koala bear are the national symbols for Australia.

There are six large species of Australian marsupials noted for hopping and bouncing on their hind legs. When the early explorers asked the Aboriginals the animal's name, the response was "I don't know." So, the explorers called them Kangaroo, or I do not know in the native language.

A Group of Kangaroos are called Mob, Court or Troupe. A Kangaroo has one stomach where a cow has 4 stomachs which means they do not belch methane gas like cattle. The little Joee jumps out of the pouch for boxing exercise and the adult male boxes and kicks for domination purposes.

When Joees are born they are lima bean sized after 31-36 days in gestation. The newborn spends another 9 months in the pouch. If during this period or if the feed of the mother is not good the gestation period can be extended. The Mother can produce two types of milk if the first baby kangaroo is in the pouch when the newborn arrives. Finally, the third leg or tail is not used for balance but is used to accelerated their

Speed. There are an estimated fifty-three million Kangaroos in Australia.

Joyce and I had now reached a new life plan and needed to reset ourselves for the future. It felt like we had just completed a marathon, and we were given an opportunity to reset our lives clear of past burdens but not clear of the lesson learned. We were two souls that needed each other with a clean start in life. But first we need a rest and get away to leave the old selves behind and look forward. We chose an extensive world travel plan that would expose us to all new life, events, places, memories and friends. Not that we wanted to lose our old friends but, at this point, we did not want to commiserate and relive the past.

7.0 First Round the World Cruise

In 2017 we had decided we truly needed a break again, so we booked a trip around the world. We realized it was going to happen when we got to San Francisco and saw our wonderful ship, The Silver Sea Whisper was sitting in the harbor. We thought we had gone to Heaven. Our estate room with a housekeeper, butler service, a well-stocked bar, balcony plus the most pleasant people and surroundings. The itinerary for our first World Cruise follows.

7.2 Highlights of First World Cruise (2017)

Dallas, USA	Georgetown, Malaysia
San Francisco, USA	Phuket, Thailand
Hilo, Maui Hawaii	Cochin, Thailand
Honolulu, Oahu Haw	Fujairah, UAE
Apia, Pacific Is	Abu Dhabi, United Arab
Nuku'alofa Poly	Emirates
Tauranga, NSW	Muscat, Oman
Gisborne, NSW Aust	Port Said, Egypt
Wellington, Australia	Alexandria, Egypt
New Plymouth, Australia	Nafplion, Greece
Tasmania, Australia	Lipari, Italy
Burnie, Australia	Monte Carlos, Monaco
Freemantle, Perth Aus	VilleFranche, France
Exmouth, Australia	Portofino, Italy
Bewang, Indonesia	Livorno, Italy
Celukan, Indonesia	Civitavecchia, Italy
Palawan, Philippines	Amalfi, Italy
Princesa, Philippines	Sorrento, Italy
Puerto, Coron,	Monos Greece
Nha Trang, S. Vietnam	Dikili, Turkey
Bangkok, Thailand	Copenhagan Denmark
Penang, Malaysia	London, England

7.2.1 China, Hong Kong Highlights

I recall landing in 1964 in the evening at Hong Kong's Suntec airport. The final glide path was between two side by side apartments. The plane was so close to the apartments you could see what they eat for dinner. There were many flights daily that repeated that landing experience.

The pilots of an Air China passenger jet at a later date lowered their altitude too soon and the plane fell in the ocean around the peninsula runway. Since the tail of the first plane was blocking further traffic in and out of Suntec and the plane was stuck in the mud, Suntec airport blew the tail off with dynamite. The plane was offloaded first and that night when the airport was closed, it was removed from mud and sea water. Next, the damaged Air China Plane was hauled to the airport gate airport where it sat for a year. This of course was not good Public Relations for Air China. For these two reasons and many others, Hong Kong built a new airport.

Since there was no room for an airport in Hong Kong due to the smallness of the country, the only way was to build an island for a new airport and runway. The Engineers took apart a mountain and built the runways and Terminal as a new island in the South China Sea. Hong Kong International is ultra-modern and opened in 1991.

The STAR ferries were the best way to get from Kowloon to the New Territories and from there I made my way to work. My responsibility was to head up a team managing the private bank branch exchanges throughout the country. I knew little about what I was doing but soon learned to get along well with the locals. This was our beginning into the cellular world. We equipped cellular towers in the tall buildings in the downtown area.

Tumbleweed 1

One feature that intrigued me was the ability to drive along the street and see the businesses on either side on your cell phone advertising their products.

Hong Kong is in the Northwest territories with an enclave in the center of it called Kowloon. It is the size of four football fields with the densest population of any city in the world with a dense population living in that space. I had a chance to visit Kowloon in 1964. Hong Kong has been governed by China, Japan and the British.

Kowloon had many illegal businesses. Doctors. hospitals, schools and businesses people profited from prostitution and drugs crimes. There are no building codes improper utilities and safety facilities. At one-point buildings were erected with so much density the light hardly reaches the ground, and lights were left on 24 hours to navigate selected streets. The air was polluted. This area of Hong Kong was known as Chinatown. Children game centers by day became apartments at night.

Japanese took down much of the wall down for Suntec runway construction and used this material to build the new airport. The Hong Kong police tried to enforce the law in the Wall city because it became a haven of crime and drugs. The city became an organized crime syndicates with crime syndicate leaders.

The British had 100-year lease on the property at Hong Kong from 1898 to 1998. At which time the British turned the colony back to the Chinese. The brothels gaming parlors and opium dens were getting shut down. Today under Chinese law enforcement, Kowloon is a much more controlled area and is being integrated with the Hong Kong northwest territories. It is an interesting section of Hong Kong to visit with all the historical changes that had been made and the hardships that the people endured. If one has an opportunity to go to Hong Kong you should visit Kowloon and get a feel for its history.

7.2.3 99 Year England's Lease is up Hong Kong China

1980s in Hong Kong marks a period when the territory was known for its wealth and trademark lifestyle. Still a crown colony (later dependent territory) of the United Kingdom. Hong Kong would be recognized internationally for its politics, entertainment and skyrocketing real estate prices. It would also go on to be the subject of intense negotiations between Britain and China, which would be resolved in the turnover from Britain to Communist China at the end of the 99 Year Lease.

7.3 Perth, Australia

We continued cruising West to Perth along the southern side of Australia or the Antarctic side. Perth was another delightful town and other than being very isolated would be a good town to live in. Continuing along the West Coast of Australia arrived at a small village called Exmouth. The Port was famous in the Second World War as it became a submarine station defending against the invading Japanese. We decided to go golfing and headed out to the local Golf course. After making reservations the taxi driver helped us. We discovered the pro shop was not open and no one was on the golf course.

We eventually found the lady that was cutting the grass and asked about getting a buggy for our golf game and paying the golf fees. The lady greens keeper of the course was not accepting our credit cards or US cash. We asked the taxi driver if he would accept a credit card, and he said yes. When he returned hours later, I used my credit card to pay for the ride and game. That trust and courtesy is characteristic of the Azzi.
Next we traveled South to Melbourne, which is a delightful mid-city-size town. The driving is on the left side of the road which was a little confusing. After spending many years living in

Singapore I had learned to drive on the left side, so I did all the driving along the coast. In fact, I had more difficulty returning to the US and adjusting to the right-hand side of the road. The trolley car is still exceedingly popular in Melbourne.

7.4 Home of the Komoto Dragons

Komoto, Indonesia, Dragons grew to maximum length of 9.8 foot, and weighing up to 150 pounds. They have a slobber coming out of their cheeks all the time. They are flesh-eating animals and are delighted in catching a deer for dinner.

The female Komoto laid, as many as twenty eggs deposited one a time in a self-dug nesting hole. The eggs are incubated for seven to 7-8 months. They take eight to nine years to mature and are estimated to live up to thirty years.

Komodo dragons also occasionally attack humans. Komodo is the only place in the world where the dragon is found in the wild. Komodo dragons have thrived in the harsh climate of Indonesia's Lesser Sunda Islands for millions of years.

7.5 Bali Indonesia

The next port on the world tour was Bali, Indonesia. Bali is visited frequently by vacationers and businesspeople from all over the world. Bali has experienced many forceful turnovers by foreign ruling powers plus explosive volcano eruptions. Tourism has drained 50 percent of the rivers and in some areas the coastline is inundated with plastic garbage. The country was once a Shangri-La (ideal community) but is now threatened by its excessive tourism.

7.5.1 Bali Women with fruit on their head

One of the ritual is for Bali Women to bring fruit to the temples as an offering and then as food for the religious leaders.

7.6 Sandakan Malaysia

Sandakan was the next port of interest. We visited the Proboscis monkey. The male monkeys are separated from the females for reasons shown below.

7.6.1 Family of Proboscis Monkeys. Photo taken by Bill Marshall

The Proboscis monkey has a large nose, a reddish-brown skin color and a long tail.

7.6.2 Thailand River Long Boat Photo taken by Bill Marshall

Long boats are narrow canoes driven by a propellor from a used engine that with an extended 20-foot drive shaft. The propeller is raised and lowered according to the depth of the water by the driver. The boat scoots through the narrow rivers carrying 10-16 passengers. It is common for other canoes carrying flowers or food and drinks for sale.

The Temples are interesting as they are very elegant with gold and silver. Each temple has a series of money bowls for contributors to their offering in, but as the coins would drop they made loud noises. The room is built to accommodate a lot of people and the noise from their coins is deafening. The thing that hits you is, keeping these temples in money as the local population is poor yet this opulence surrounds them. Consequently, tourism is especially important.

Bill Marshall

8.0 Second Round the Word Cruise

We enjoyed the first Round the world trip so much that in another 18 months in 2019 we took a second Word Cruise to different ports and countries. Joyce and I loved the arrangements for the Voyage as we knew the ship line, Silversea and the ship Whisperer. It felt like going home with our second round-the-world cruise. Many of the cruise directors and management were friends. We ended up having a wonder full time on both Cruises and making new friends.

My responsibilities for Real Estate back home were met and all decisions, communications, and upkeep items were transacted via the Ship to Shore provided facilities. We had a live-in house sitter for security in Denton Texas. These arrangements made us feel that our responsibilities back home were taken care of. We were to be gone 135 days visiting 38 countries and 43 ports.

8.1 Itinerary

The following was the itinerary for the second round the world cruises and a few side trips. Following this outline are the memories from our voyage. We made friends on board with the crew and many of the passengers that we correspond with today.

Fort Lauderdale, USA	Chilean Fjords, Chile
Cartagena, Colombia	Garibaldi Fjord, Chile
Panama Canal Transit	Ushuaia, Argentina
Puntarenas, Costa Rica	Drake Passage Antartica
Po Quepos, Costa Rica	Antarctic Peninsula
Guayaquil, Ecuador	South Georgia, Georgia
Arica, Chile	Sandwich islands
Antofagasta, Chile	Tristan Cunha St Helena
Valparaíso, Chile	Mossel, South Africa
Puerto Montt, Chile	Port Elizabeth, S Africa

Richards Bay, S Africa
Durban, South África
Maputo, Mozambique
Zanzibar, Tanzania
La Digue, Seychelles
Mahe, Seychelles
Jeddah, Saudi Arabia
Dubai, Saudi Arabia
Safaga (Luxor), Egypt
Aqaba (Petra)
Suez Canal
Ashdod Israel
Haifa, Israel
Antalya, Turkey
Rhodes, Greece
Hisada's, Turkey
Dardanelles, Turkey
Istanbul, Turkey
Athens Greece
Siracusa, Turkey
Valletta, Malta
Malaga, Spain
Tangier, Morocco
Sevilla, Spain
Lisbon, Portugal
Oporto Portugal
La Corina, Spain
Jeddah, Saudi Arabia
Dhiba, Saudi Arabia
Safaga (Luxor), Egypt
Aqaba (Petra)
Suez Canal
Ashdod Israel
Haifa, Israel

Antalya, Turkey
Rhodes, Greece
Hisada's, Turkey
Dardanelles, Turkey
Istanbul, Turkey

Antalya, Turkey
Rhodes, Greece
Hisada's, Turkey
Dardanelles, Turkey
Istanbul, Turkey
Bilbao, Spain
Bordeaux, France
Saint Marlo
Southampton, UK
Falmouth, UK
Cardiff, UK
Dublin Ireland
Belfast, UK
Portree, UK
Reykjavik, Iceland
Bergan, Norway
Kristain Norway
Oslo, Norway
Aalborg, Denmark
Copenhagen Denmark

8.2 Nha Trang, South Vietnam

When I lived in Nha Trang the streets were narrow and very dirty paths. Many houses were built of sheets of corrugated tin to made a shack. Today it is a bustling Seaside touristy city.

Rickshaws have given way to cars and motorcycles on the paved streets. I recall sitting at a side street restaurant table, waiting for my soup when a big spider came out from their home under the table and collected crumbs off the table. I got up and told the waiter I changed my order to, "take out".

When the town got occupied by the communist army from the north in 1968 the big white Buda statue in the center of Nha Trang was peppered with bullet holes. Today, there is no sign of turmoil. Earlier in the book I described a scene from an afternoon on Hong Tray Island. Today the very site is a carnival park and no sign that says, "Bill's staff party was here in 1967".

8.3 Abu Dhabi United Arab Emirates

"Abu" is Arabic for father, and "Dhabi" is the Arabic word for gazelle. Abu Dhabi means "Father of Gazelle." The Gazelle is the national symbol for the UAE-United Arab Republic. The UAE has the most advanced and developed city in the region.

Joyce and I visited the UAE in 2017 and saw some spectacular sights and learned more about the United Arab Emirates. The UAE is a elected monarchy formed from a federation of seven emirates in 1973.
The temperatures rise to 123F, and blinding sandstorms occur every year. The pearl diving business was a key industry prior to the discovery of oil reserves. Oil demand continued to grow to the benefit of the Persian Gulf.

8.3.1 Burg Khalifa World Tallest Building
In 2009, the UAE set a new world record for the tallest cantilever building in the world record as it opened the One Za'abeel twin skyscrapers. The Burg Khalifa opened in 2009 as the tallest building structure in the world. Silver Sea Cruse took us to the top of the Burg Khalifa for cocktails on the top of the 124 floor. Following that we went to dinner and saw live camels as part of the performance and the Whirling Dervish.

8.4 Suez Egypt
The Suez Canal is a human-made waterway that cuts north-south across the Isthmus of Suez in Egypt. The Suez Canal in Egypt connects the Mediterranean Sea to the Red Sea, making it the shortest maritime route to Asia from Europe. Since its completion in 1869, it has become one of the world's most heavily used shipping lanes.

The time saved by the passage is almost invaluable. Today it would take a ship 3 days to travel from a port in Italy to India, for instance, and covering a distance of around four thousand four hundred nautical miles, if it passed through the Suez Canal.
The second quickest way to complete that same journey would be via the Cape of Good Hope and around Africa. At the same speed, it would take three weeks to traverse the route, which is ten thousand nautical miles longer.

The original Suez was built over the course of 10 years by local peasants drafted and forced into labor, and European workers. The Suez had been shut down for eight years from 1967 due to a border dispute between a warring Egypt and Israel, a conflict that left more than a dozen ships, known as the Yellow Fleet, trapped in the canal for the duration.

8.4.1 Suez Cannel

Suez Cannel Photo by Bill Marshall

More than 80% of global trade by volume is moved by sea, and disruptions are adding billions of dollars to supply chain costs. Globally, the average cost to ship a 40-foot container shot up from $1,040 from June to $4,570 with the detour around Africa.

There were many stoppages in the building of the original channel due to hostilities from all sides. Due to the increasing demand for use of the canal the newly expanded canal allowed a second lane to reduce the wait time for ships.

8.4.2 Cargo Ship in the Suez

The new Suez Cannel opened in 2015 at a cost of nine billion. Today three billion dollars of cargo transit the hundred-mile channel each day from Port Said in the Mediterranean to the Red sea and the Indian Ocean.

8.6 Acaba Jorden

Lawrence of Arabia fought against the Turks in World War One. He and a small troop from the UK shut down a land route from Acaba on the Red Sea to Syria on The Mediterranean Sea.
Lawrence a Lieutenant in the British military knocked out 70 roads and railway bridges. This stopped the military supplies from the Atlantic and Pacific areas reaching Europe.

He was an unassuming young Englishman, who found himself the champion of a downtrodden people, thrust into events that changed the course of history. Lawrence and his troops attacked a troop train just south of Acaba, destroying a locomotive and killing some 70 Turkish soldiers.

His wartime memoir was his best-seller in the books, "Seven Pillars of Wisdom."

Joyce and I decided to play 18 holes of golf when we docked in Acaba Jordan. The in-town course was beautiful and for some reason we had the course all to ourselves. We looked around the town before returning to the ship.

We were having a refreshment at 5:30 pm back on the ship when we heard the loud boom and felt a vibration from an explosion. We could see a trail of black smoke from close by explosion and fire truck sirens headed our way at the docks.

We learned that a drone from the Hothi rebels in Yemen had delivered a bomb and dropped it a short distance away from our ship at a fuel storage area. Yemen is a sovereign state in West Asia. Located in the Southern Arabian Peninsula, it borders.

Saudi Arabia. The Hothi are unfriendly towards Saudi Arabia and other bordering countries and at this point have overtaken the government in Yemen, but control or at least disrupt the sea traffic into the Red Sea towards the Suez Canal.

Our Captain realized it was not a safe harbor and began to leave port. We left behind was a zodiac craft boat to bring the remaining passengers to the ship outside the harbor. Everything quieted down after that, and we got on the way to our next port.

8.7 Istanbul Turkey

Istanbul straddles the Bosporus Strait, the boundary between Asia & Europe

8.7.1 Blue Mosque Photo from Wikipedia, free

The Blue Mosque is famous for its blue tiles which adorns its interior. It was originally built in the early 16th century most iconic and popular monuments of the Ottoman architecture. The mosque was built next to the former Hippodrome and stands across from the Hagia Sophia, another popular tourist site. The 6 golden Minarets announce the Moslem prayers 5 times daily

8.7.2 Istanbul Grand Bazaar Photo from Wikipedia, free

Istanbul straddles the Bosporus Strait, the boundary between Asia and Europe with over 25 Million residents.

The Istanbul Bazaar is one of the largest and oldest covered markets in the world, with 61 covered streets and over 4,000 shops. Over 100 Million tourists visit the Bazar each year. The method of trade is bargaining.

I will describe my experience with bargaining in Turkey. Joyce and I were leaving the Bazaar and was approached by young man with prayer rugs over his shoulder. He said "one hundred dollars each" for his carpets as they were silk. I knew this price was too cheap for a silk product but too expensive for a non-silk fabric. I told the young man that we are visitors with no room to carry such a rug to the USA.

But the young man persisted and followed us down street to our waiting bus. All the way he kept lowering his price so as we got on the bus we finally agreed to twenty-five dollars. When we got home some months later I had a yellow nightlight, and I saw streaks of silk in the rug. So, I finally confirmed, I got a good buy. Today that prayer mat sits on the floor at the foot of our bed. I think of the story as I get ready for bed.

8.7 Seville, Spain
Seville, located in the heart of Spain has a rich history of medieval to modern times. What intrigued us was the 200-mile river ride in our ocean-going cruise ship. The river had been obviously dredged out, but it felt at times you could reach out and touch the Spanish countryside.

The ship just fits in the lift locks as we cruised east towards Seville.

8.1 Seville Spain 200-mile river Cruise Photo by Bill Marshall

After attending a Seville country Fair highlighting horses and period costumed people we spent the rest of the evening on the river in a tranquil setting. The ship did a 360 turn and was ready to Cruise back to the Atlantic Ocean. The next day, after a morning in Saville, we returned back to the wonderful views in our private ship (felt private). We were mesmerized by our journey to Saville Spain.

Did I mention that for the entire journey no matter where we were in the world we always slept in the same bed and did not have to repack. This is the advantage of cruising the world.

Bill Marshall

9.0 Change career path

In early 2022 I continued with my Real Estate Broker license but reduced my activities to a retirement level of business. By September of 2022, I officially retired at age 79.

Tumbleweed Book 2 anticipated publishing date is sometime in 2025..

9.1 We are enjoying our anniversary

Bill Marshall

Tumbleweed 1

Appendix A

There were 29 homes in Bill's Life

Location	Area	Comment	Year
Port Hope	S Ontario	Born	10/04/1943
Goodwood	C Ontario	Parsonage	1946-1947
Goodwood	C Ontario	Country	1947-1949
Waubaushiene	N Ontario	Cottage	1950-1952
Cannington	C Ontario	Parsonage	1952-1953
Cannington	C Ontario	Train Station	1953-1955
Seaforth	W Ontario	Train Station	1957-1958
Markham	C Ontario	Main St	1957-1958
Streeter	C Illinois	Fed Electric	1961-1961
Tuktoyaktuk	Yukon	Dew Line	1961-1964
Pleiku	S Vietnam	MAC V HQ	1964-1966
Dalat	S Vietnam	Mountain	1966-1967
Nha Trang	S Vietnam	S China Sea	1967-1968
Markham	C Ontario	Winlaw Pl	1968-1974
Sudbury	N Ontario	Blezard Valley	1974-1977
Oshawa	S Ontario	Address	1977-1979
McLean	Virginia	Route 66	1979-1982
Reston	Virginia	Fairfax	1981-1984
Plano	N Texas	Bender	1984-1990
Singapore	Orchard St		1990-1992
Singapore	New Tec Park		1992-1997
Plano	N Texas	Park & Coit	1997-2001
Lake Lavon	N Texas	RV Park	2000-2001
Whitney	C Texas	Lake Whitney	2001-2004
Justin	N Texas	RV Church	2004-2005
Denton	N Texas	Crestview	2005-2008
Denton	N Texas	Landmark Ln	2008-2024

Bill Marshall is available for interviews. For more information send requests to info@advbooks.com

advbookstore.com
we bring dreams to life™

www.ingramcontent.com/pod-product-compliance
Lightning Source LLC
LaVergne TN
LVHW051704080426
835511LV00017B/2729